Countryside

The Countryside

of England, Wales, and Northern Ireland

Photographs by

Joe Cornish, David Noton

and Paul Wakefield

Introduction by Richard Mabey

Harry N. Abrams, Inc., Publishers

First published in Great Britain in 1998 by
National Trust Enterprises Ltd,
36 Queen Anne's Gate, London SW1H 9AS

Distributed in 1998 by Harry N. Abrams, Incorporated, New York

British Library Cataloguing in Publication Data
A catalogue record for this book is available from the British Library.

ISBN 0 7078 0244 X (hardback)
ISBN 0 7078 0269 5 (paperback, available in 1999)
ISBN 0-8109-6361-2 (Abrams)

Captions compiled by Margaret Willes, the National Trust's Publisher,
with the help of Jo Burgon, Coast and Countryside Adviser,
Richard Offen, Enterprise Neptune Appeal Manager,
Katherine Hearn, Nature Conservation Adviser,
and individual property staff.

Picture research by the National Trust Photographic Library
Edited by Helen Fewster
Designed and typeset in Carter Cone Galliard by Peter and Alison Guy
Production management by Bob Towell
Printed and bound in China
Phoenix Offset

Frontispiece: The chimneys and thatched roofs of SELWORTHY, part of the
Holnicote Estate in Somerset. Sir Thomas Acland rebuilt the village for his
estate pensioners in 1828 and planted trees in the steep valley and on the hill to
produce 'natural countryside' that is in fact totally contrived by man. [DN]

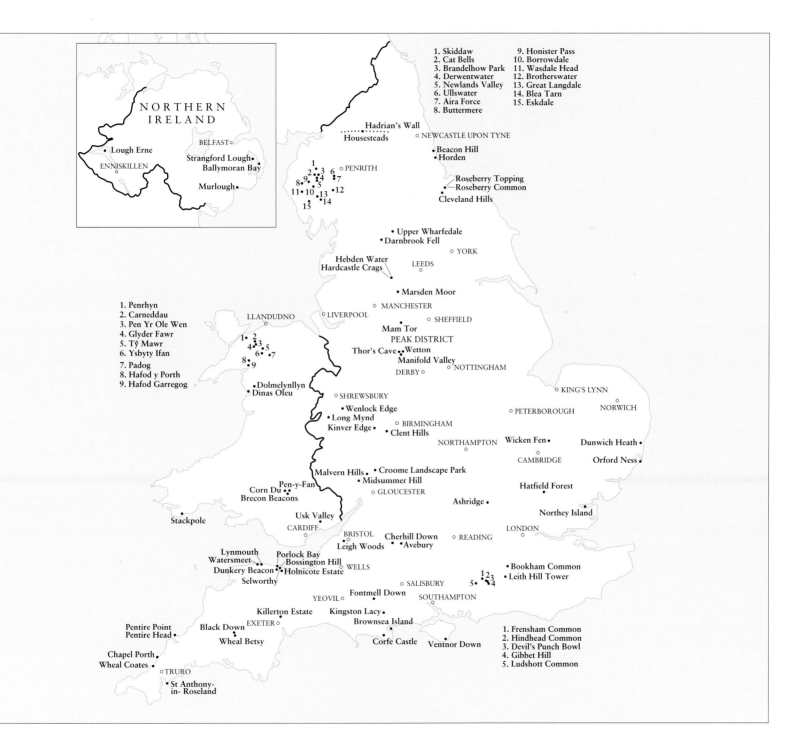

NORTHERN IRELAND

Lough Erne
BELFAST
ENNISKILLEN
Strangford Lough
Ballymoran Bay
Murlough

1. Skiddaw
2. Cat Bells
3. Brandelhow Park
4. Derwentwater
5. Newlands Valley
6. Ullswater
7. Aira Force
8. Buttermere
9. Honister Pass
10. Borrowdale
11. Wasdale Head
12. Brotherswater
13. Great Langdale
14. Blea Tarn
15. Eskdale

1. Penrhyn
2. Carneddau
3. Pen Yr Ole Wen
4. Glyder Fawr
5. Tŷ Mawr
6. Ysbyty Ifan
7. Padog
8. Hafod y Porth
9. Hafod Garregog

Hadrian's Wall
Housesteads
NEWCASTLE UPON TYNE
Beacon Hill
Horden
PENRITH
Roseberry Topping
Roseberry Common
Cleveland Hills

Upper Wharfedale
Darnbrook Fell
YORK
Hebden Water
Hardcastle Crags
LEEDS
Marsden Moor

LLANDUDNO
LIVERPOOL
MANCHESTER
SHEFFIELD
Mam Tor
PEAK DISTRICT
Thor's Cave Wetton
Manifold Valley
DERBY
NOTTINGHAM

Dolmelynllyn
Dinas Oleu
SHREWSBURY
Wenlock Edge
Long Mynd
Kinver Edge
BIRMINGHAM
Clent Hills
NORTHAMPTON
KING'S LYNN
NORWICH
PETERBOROUGH
Wicken Fen
Dunwich Heath
CAMBRIDGE
Orford Ness

Malvern Hills
Croome Landscape Park
Midsummer Hill
Pen-y-Fan
Corn Du
Brecon Beacons
GLOUCESTER
Ashridge
Hatfield Forest
Northey Island
LONDON

Stackpole
Usk Valley
CARDIFF
BRISTOL
Cherill Down
Leigh Woods Avebury
READING
Bookham Common
Leith Hill Tower

Lynmouth
Watersmeet
Porlock Bay
Bossington Hill
Dunkery Beacon Holnicote Estate
Selworthy
WELLS
SALISBURY
Fontmell Down
SOUTHAMPTON

1. Frensham Common
2. Hindhead Common
3. Devil's Punch Bowl
4. Gibbet Hill
5. Ludshott Common

YEOVIL
Killerton Estate
Kingston Lacy
Pentire Point
Pentire Head
Black Down
EXETER
Wheal Betsy
Brownsea Island
Corfe Castle
Ventnor Down

Chapel Porth
Wheal Coates
TRURO
St Anthony-in- Roseland

Introduction by Richard Mabey

The popular movement for access to the countryside has marched almost step for step with the development of landscape photography. When the Ingleton Scenery Company opened up the country's first scenic reserve in the Yorkshire Dales in 1885, the Gibson family were already creating their extraordinary forensic images of the Scilly Isles, in which giant cider presses took on the look of megaliths, and Celtic field boundaries of garden hedges. In 1895, the very year the National Trust was formed, the Kearton brothers published their first historic portraits of birds in their own miniature landscapes – their habitats. The coincidence wasn't really surprising: we were hungry not just to go back to our heartlands, but to probe their innermost meanings.

These celebratory explorations have gone on hand in hand, and it is fitting that this portfolio of photographs of some of the wildest, most beautiful and historically rich places in the English, Welsh and Northern Irish countryside should be of the properties of that champion of public access, the National Trust. Joe Cornish, David Noton and Paul Wakefield have tracked across the vast and intricate range of landscapes which the Trust protects, from snowed-up cornices in Snowdonia to the lush summer marshes of Wicken Fen in Cambridgeshire – all of them as accessible to the public as to the lens.

Yet for all the continuity in these twin traditions, there is something subtly new about this generation of countryside images – and something which has little to do with the awesome advances in photographic technology that have occurred over the past century. It has to do with the way we *look* at pictures and the places they represent, and at our place in them.

Photography in the Victorian period was energised with scientific and sociological curiosity, with a sense of the power achieved by knowledge and possession (even today, we still 'capture' a photographic likeness), and with a belief that through it we could come closer to the heart of what we saw as our greatest and most defining national resource. If the camera did not lie and – as they said – the truth set you free, those penetrating glares into the distant

The photographer in his element. Joe Cornish's assistant, Chrissie Lane, on the summit of GLYDER FACH, Carneddau in North Wales. [JC]

Left: Autumnal mist over the LONG MYND in Shropshire. [JC]

green (the sharper the better) could be a way towards a true democracy of the countryside. As early as 1844 the pioneer William Henry Fox Talbot had dreamed of what might be achieved by the accuracy and *fixedness* of the photographic image:

> to reflect on the inimitable beauty of the pictures of nature's painting which the glass lens of the Camera throws upon the paper in its focus – fairy pictures, creatures of a moment, and destined rapidly to fade away... how charming it would be if it were possible to cause these natural images to imprint themselves durably, and remain fixed upon the paper.
>
> *The Pencil of Nature*

That durability was to become one of the greatest assets of photography. The brief glimpse could become a permanent archive.

But by the early years of the twentieth century, both professional landscape photographers and the increasing army of amateurs making their way into the hills and fields with their box cameras were discovering that photographs did not just 'fix' scenes: in our imaginations, they could also liberate them. Each image reminded you of what had been there seconds, minutes before; of what might be there later, when the bird had flown, the sun set, the leaves fallen. They were part of an almost infinite series of possibilities – of close-ups, prospects, shifts of light; of patterns of labour and the slow workings of geology; of quick glances and long meditations. And, for that matter, of muffed shots, raindrops on the lens and wind-shaken tripods – all the animated chaos of the interaction between photographer and countryside. Photography 'catches', when we read it sensitively, the vitality and unpredictability of the living landscape. And for today's increasingly photo-literate snappers, even the most sharply focused scenes are redolent of Wordsworth's vision of a landscape teeming and unbiddable and, in the best way, fuzzy at the edges. And it is all ours. Landscape photography is, in a sense, a new right of common. As Wordsworth said, 'a wilderness is rich with liberty'.

So it is apt that this collection begins in Wordsworth's Cumbria, where the National Trust acquired some of its first countryside properties. These are archetypal pictures of an ancient human presence in a turbulent landscape. Mist rises over Blea Tarn. The ice at the edge of Derwentwater forms cobweb patterns like contour lines. And in David Noton's wide and airy panorama of Loughrigg Tarn you are *in* the water-lilies, up to your knees, with the faintest breeze blurring the tops of the sedges.

An intriguing view of the PEAK DISTRICT in Derbyshire: autumn colours reflected in flood waters near the Ladybower Reservoir. [JC]

Left: NEWLANDS VALLEY in Cumbria, from the ridge of Catbells, with Bassenthwaite in the distance. [JC]

The delicate beauty of winter: (*far left*) ice formations on the river below LLYN IDWAL in Carneddau; HEBDEN WATER (*left*) in West Yorkshire. [JC]

There are so many ways in which the capriciousness, the presence of nature interacts with the old rhythms and sense of historical continuity that give us our sense of place. The limbs of the ancient yew trees near Crom Old Castle in Northern Ireland are a thousand years old, but look as frisky and voluptuous as teenagers basking on a beach. A lake of bluebells floods a patch of downland on the Isle of Wight, the 'ghost' of what was probably once a wood. And everywhere the great set pieces of prospect and view remind you of the deep seated and common patterns of evolution in the natural world. Wind-blown snow on the summit of Pen Yr Ole Wen has the look of surf breaking on a shoreline. The 'river' at Croome Park in Herefordshire shot from low down, looks poised to one day reclaim Capability Brown's trim landscape. A view of a harvest field at Cherhill Down, Wiltshire, contains almost the entire sweep of European agricultural history, from late twentieth-century bales back to the outlines of an archetypal horse carved in the chalk. And Joe Cornish's long-focus view of the shingle ridges of Orford Ness in Suffolk reminds you of an immense cross-section of the annular rings of a tree.

These pictures, arranged as a roughly anti-clockwise tour of England, Wales and Northern Ireland, take in the compressed variety of our countryside and the ways it has been shaped both by nature and humans – the Trust included. If there are few actual humans shown in the collection it is because they are always there implicitly in the landscape: in the ancient troglodyte dwellings in the red sandstone cliffs at Kinver Edge, Staffordshire; in the dry-stone walls on Cowside in Yorkshire, whose swirls and strata echo natural limestone formations; in the chequerboard of farmland round Bossington in Exmoor that will be given back voluntarily to the rising sea.

And there is one other persistent human presence – you, the viewer. The reader of a landscape image brings to it not just a reaction to its intense vision of the present, but to the echoes of history engrained in it, and to the unpredictable and exciting future that unravels from that moment when they were 'taken'.

Detail of bark on a horse chestnut tree on the ASHRIDGE ESTATE in Hertfordshire. [PW]

Previous page: DERWENTWATER, looking towards Catbells. This is quintessential Lake District landscape, cherished by millions of visitors who come to admire and enjoy it in every season. [JC]

Popularity has its price: not only is the Cumbrian landscape cherished, it is threatened too. In the early nineteenth century William Wordsworth was concerned about summer homes of Manchester businessmen appearing on the shores of Windermere. In his *Guide to the Lakes*, published in 1810, he suggested the area be designated 'a sort of national property in which every man has a right and interest who has an eye to perceive and a heart to enjoy'.

This theme was taken up eighty years later by the founders of the National Trust, Octavia Hill, Robert Hunter, and Hardwicke Rawnsley, Vicar of Crosthwaite and guiding spirit behind the Lake District Defence Society. One of Rawnsley's early, successful campaigns was against the building by slate quarry owners of a railway to the heart of Borrowdale. *Right:* An abandoned slate quarry on HONISTER PASS, with Buttermere in the distance. [JC]

Far right: DERWENT ISLE on Derwentwater. Responding to Wordsworth's concern about ugly development, the National Trust bought Brandelhow Park on Derwentwater in 1902 by public subscription. Octavia Hill wrote, 'you can see the whole space of the lake set with its island, it has crags and meadows and wood, on it the sun shines, over it the wind blows, it will be preserved in its present loveliness and it belongs to you all and to every landless man, woman and child in England'. [JC]

: 18 : During its long geological history, the Lake District has been mountain range, clear sea, swamp and desert, but it took on its present form during the last Ice Age, when glaciers gouged out its valleys and created the lakes.

There are sixteen major lakes, ranging from huge Windermere, ten and a half miles in length, to Brothers-water, less than half a mile long. The National Trust protects over one-third of the Lake District National Park, some 140,000 acres, almost 60,000 ha.

Previous pages: A magnificent panorama of the lakes from Caudale Moor, with BROTHERSWATER in the middle distance, and ULLSWATER beyond. [JC]

Right: Fells in shadow, BUTTERMERE VALLEY. Enjoyment of the high places has always been part of the Lake District's attraction, and the National Park now receives over twelve million visits annually. One of the main tasks shouldered by the National Trust is coping with footpath erosion and repair, with teams of full-time workers supported by volunteers. [JC]

For early tourists, especially eighteenth-century travellers, the Lakes represented Nature in the raw, with awful landscapes enhanced in their awfulness by Claude glasses, piano-convex mirrors which miniaturised the view and tinted it to resemble an engraving. But man has long left his mark upon this apparently natural landscape, especially in farming patterns.

Farms were sited in valley bottoms, with fields climbing to the limit of the good ground and known as *inbye* land. Above were the open fells, where the hardy Herdwick sheep could graze at will, being *heafed*, naturally remaining in a defined area. In 1943, the children's writer Beatrix Potter stipulated in her will that the farms she left to the National Trust should be let at a moderate rent and that the landlord's flocks of sheep on the fell farms should be pure Herdwick in breed. *Above:* A Herdwick grazing in the early morning mist by BLEA TARN, Eskdale. [DN]

Right: The lakes are rich in resources. Their clear, clean water, allows unusual fish like the charr to live in their depths. The smallest member of the salmon family, the charr is now very difficult to find because it is not fished commercially, but it tastes delicious. In the late seventeenth century, Daniel Fleming of Ryedale wrote that Coniston Water produced 'many pikes or Jacks, Bass or Perch, Trouts, Eels and Charrs; which last is much esteemed and valued'. This photograph shows DERWENTWATER at dawn. [DN]

: 22 : ULLSWATER, one of the 'eastern protectorates of the Trust's Lake District Empire' according to the *National Trust Guide*. In 1911 the threat of building development spurred the Trust to buy Gowbarrow Park, a medieval deer park with the picturesque waterfall of Aira Force, on the west side of the lake. Additional acquisitions now mean that the National Trust owns the south quarter of Ullswater, forever linked with Wordsworth's famous lines, 'I wandered lonely as a cloud'. [DN]

Man has not only left his agricultural mark on the Lake District land-scape, he has also 'improved' nature. Perhaps the most well-known example is Tarn Hows, an artificial lake created and planted in the Swiss style in Victorian times. GRISEDALE near Patterdale (*above*) is also a designed landscape. Although it escaped the fate of becoming a reservoir for Manchester, its natural deciduous woodland planting was 'improved' with the addition of blocks of conifer. This environ-mentally damaging practice is, luckily, on the decline. [DN]

Right: AIRA FORCE, cascading down to Ullswater. The natural features of the waterfall were enhanced in the early nineteenth century. [DN]

The delta at the head of WASDALE is a flat plain across which several streams flow on their way to the lake. The vegetation is tussocky purple moor grass mire, a valuable area for marsh plants. Where the land has been put to agriculture the fields are divided by dry-stone walling. Originally cattle were grazed here, now it is almost entirely sheep farming. [JC]

LOUGHRIGG TARN, at the foot of Great Langdale, near Ambleside. One of the more nutrient rich of the hundreds of pools, lakes and tarns scattered liberally across the Lake District fells, Loughrigg can support white water-lilies and a rich aquatic vegetation. Sedges and spikes of purple loosestrife form a fringe of plants around the edge of the water, important for dragonflies. [DN]

MURLOUGH in Dundrum Bay on the coast of County Down, was designated Northern Ireland's first national nature reserve in 1977. The range of sand dunes, formed over 5,000 years ago, has been inhabited since Neolithic times, and traces of dwellings and implements regularly turn up as the wind shifts the sand.

Right: The National Trust has planted marram grass to stabilise the sand dunes, relying on the mobility of the fresh sand to encourage growth. [PW]

Once stabilised, the dunes take on a grey, dense appearance as they become colonised by other plants (*above*). [JC]

Previous pages: STRANGFORD is one of the largest sea loughs in Northern Ireland, a marine inlet created by inundation of the landscape as the Ice Age sheets melted. The lough channel is over twenty miles in length, and contains more than a hundred tiny islands known as drumlins, semi-submerged flying saucers that were the deposits dumped by the retreating ice sheets. They provide a rich shoreline for a huge and varied number of plant and animal species. Strangford is particularly famous as the over-wintering ground for duck and goose, and for summer breeding of terns. [JC]

Because of this wealth of wildlife, the lough is a marine nature reserve, with the various organisations that own the foreshore working together to ensure there are sanctuary areas for the wildlife.

Right: BALLYMORAN BAY at sunrise with the mudflats exposed. This intertidal zone has been leased by the National Trust from the Crown Estate. *Left:* The sun reflected in a tidal pool on the foreshore. [JC]

While Strangford is a sea lough, on the east coast of Northern Ireland, LOUGH ERNE is an inland lough, part of the CROM ESTATE, lying at the very western edge, in County Fermanagh. The lough is linked up to the Shannon, and is a popular site for visitors with boats. *Far right:* The National Trust has provided places to park, and facilities for the hire of boats at Crom and Enniskillen, but also has to try to preserve the tranquillity of the place. [JC]

The Crom Estate, spread over 1,900 acres (770 ha), is a patchwork of land and water with little wooded islands, mostly of oak. Lord Erne continues to live in the New Castle, built in 1832–8 by Edward Blore, while the National Trust looks after the Old Castle, a seventeenth-century tower house, and various other eye-catchers in the park. *Above:* Crom Castle boathouse. [JC]

Detail of sulphur polypore fungus on a fallen tree in the woodland on Inisherk Island, Crom. Fallen trees are deliberately left to decay, so that fungi and insects can thrive on their dead wood. [JC]

An ancient yew near Crom Old Castle – possibly over a thousand years old. [JC]

CARNEDDAU is a spectacular mountain range in Snowdonia National Park in North Wales. It came to the National Trust in 1951 as part of the endowment for the Penrhyn Estate, so mountains created in the Ice Age were donated to support the upkeep of a Victorian castle.

Far right: The ridge of GLYDER FAWR, with snow-capped hills in the distance. [JC]

Right: Constant frost action over the centuries has produced a plateau on the summit of PEN YR OLE WEN, over which the winter winds blow the snow in dramatic formations. [JC]

: 42 : Frost action at work in the Carneddau. Despite this hostile environment, lichens and moss survive on the rocks.

Right: Snow-covered ice formations on the river below Llyn Idwal, with Y GARN looking out of the mist. [JC]

Far right: The sun setting over sheet ice, looking towards Y Garn, with PEN YR OLE WEN to the right. [JC]

Previous pages: A bright winter's day in the CARNEDDAU, looking towards, left to right, Tryfan, Glyder Fach and Y Garn. The glacial formation has created a U-shaped cwm with a lake. Here Alpine flora flourish, including the Snowdon lily, while sheep from six high valley farms graze the mountain slopes. Carneddau is home, too, to thousands of visitors, drawn by the mountaineering and rock climbing, the classic mountain geomorphology, and the glorious scenery. [JC]

The Penrhyn Estate consists of 36,700 acres (14,860 ha), the largest owned by the National Trust. It comes in three parts: Carneddau, Tŷ Mawr and YSBYTY IFAN. In comparison with the icy peaks of Carneddau, the hills and valleys of Ysbyty are gentle, with villages and hill sheep farms. Nevertheless the farming here is on marginal land, with the Trust supporting the farmers to retain the environment by giving them extra income through hedge-laying and dry-stone walling.

Above: Looking south to PEN-Y-GENLAN from Bryn Bras Farm. [JC]

Right: A footbridge over Afon Eidda at PADOG. [JC]

: 48 : Dry-stone walls surround the ancient woodlands of HAFOD GARREGOG, an area of about 420 acres (170 ha) of undisturbed countryside near the Aberglaslyn Pass in Snowdonia. The woods and wetlands provide the habitat for the rare Silver Studded Blue Butterfly which exists nowhere else in the area and has probably been isolated here since the last Ice Age. [JC]

Far right: The typical subdivisions of a Snowdonian hill farm can clearly be seen at HAFOD Y PORTH. The open mountain gives way to the enclosed *ffridd*, rough grazing, below the mountain wall. Ancient oak woods grow on the less exposed rocky parts of the farm and the level ground has been cultivated.

In the centre of the lower parts of the farm is the rocky hill of Dinas Emrys, the site of an ancient British fort. The scene of many legends, it is the home of the Welsh Dragon. [JC]

Left: The steep, gorse-clad fell of DINAS OLEU, Gwynedd, the National Trust's first property. Four and a half acres came to the Trust only weeks after the organisation's official formation in 1895, given by Fanny Talbot to prevent the spread of the seaside town of Barmouth along the coast. Octavia Hill's reaction to Mrs Talbot's generosity was to note, 'We have got our first piece of property, I wonder if it will be the last'. Little did she know. [JC]

Above: The DOLMELYNLLYN ESTATE lies in the upper part of the Mawddach Valley, one of Snowdonia's best kept secrets. The National Trust has provided a way-marked footpath through ancient oak woodland, past the dramatic Rhaeadr Ddu waterfall to the melancholy remains of a gold mine. [DN]

STACKPOLE in Dyfed. For three centuries this estate in South Wales, looking out over the Atlantic, was owned by the Scottish Earls of Cawdor. In *Macbeth* Shakespeare alludes to the prosperity of the Thane of Cawdor, and this prosperity can be seen at Stackpole, where the family landscaped the estate by planting woodlands and damming valleys to make freshwater lakes.

Above: One of the lakes, now part of a National Nature Reserve and well-known for its water-lilies. [JC]

Right: Trees overlooking the lake. [JC]

Previous pages: The red sandstone of the BRECON BEACONS makes for a much more open landscape than Snowdonia, and man has long inhabited even the peaks. Neolithic and Bronze Age relics have been found, along with inscribed stones dating from the fifth and sixth centuries when this area formed part of the Irish principality of Brycheiniog. This photograph looks from Craig Cwareli west towards Pen-y-Fan and Cribyn. [JC]

The Brecon Beacons are now a National Park, just one valley across from the mining valleys, and thus a playground for South Wales.

Above: So many walkers use the footpaths that they have become badly eroded. [JC]

Right: The land is farmed for sheep, with open fields and no walls, because the sandstone is not suitable. Looking south west from Llechfaen, over the Usk Valley to the Beacons. [JC]

The PEAK DISTRICT, spreading across Derbyshire, Staffordshire and Yorkshire, is completely surrounded by the great industrial cities of the North and Midlands of England. DOVEDALE, in the South Peak, for instance, has to accommodate more than two million visitors each year, staunchly fulfilling Octavia Hill's desire to provide an open-air lung for town dwellers.

This is limestone country, good for walking and climbing, with a subterranean landscape for caving, and the River Dove a place of pilgrimage for anglers since Izaak Walton wrote the *Compleat Angler* in 1653.
Above: The crags of Bunster Hill, from the summit of Thorpe Cloud. [JC] *Right:* Looking south-west over farmland from South Head Hill. [JC]

Right: Thor's Cave, one of the spectacular limestone caves in the MANIFOLD VALLEY. Excavations in the nineteenth century confirmed that it was in use in Romano-British times, while investigations in neighbouring caves have revealed flints and animal bones from the Upper Palaeolithic period, twelve thousand years ago. [DN]

Far right: Farmland near WETTON, in the South Peak. Taking advantage of the limestone, the fields are divided by dry-stone walls. The field barn is designed to store hay in the upper part and to house livestock below. [JC]

: 62 : MAM TOR in the Dark Peak. Mam Tor is known as the shivering mountain because of continual landslips over the centuries: its east face now looks like a gigantic quarry. This gritstone landscape is grim and ancient, with evidence of prehistoric barrows. It is also superb walking country, with wonderful views: this picture looks north-east along the ridge to Hollins Cross, Back Tor and Lose Hill Pike. [JC]

KINVER EDGE in Staffordshire is a prominent sandstone escarpment. From the top there are dramatic views of Shropshire and the Clent Hills (p.70), but equally striking are the dwellings cut into the soft stone of the Edge itself. The earliest records of these houses date back to the seven-teenth century, and by the end of the last century upwards of one hundred people were living in Kinver Edge. The cave dwellers fitted their accommodation with all the comforts they could acquire, taking advantage of the warmth in winter and enjoying the cool in summer. [JC]

The Kinver dwellings were abandoned in the early 1960s when some of the upper levels with brick frontages were demolished. The National Trust has recently recreated the top tier to enable a warden to offer twenty-four hour protection to the site from vandals. [JC]

The LONG MYND in Shropshire is a great ridge, running some ten miles from south-west to north-east, separating England and Wales – mynd is probably derived from the Welsh *mynydd* for mountain. The ridge is made up of some of the oldest rocks in England, pre-Cambrian shale, creating a landscape of steep valleys known as hollows or batches. For centuries this has been common-land, heavily grazed by sheep.

  Along the spine of the ridge runs the Portway, originally a Bronze Age route, later used by cattle drovers bringing their animals from North Wales through to market in the English Midlands and South.

Trying to cross the Long Mynd on a winter's day can be a dangerous experience, as proved by the Rev. Carr who, on 29 January 1865 set out to return from a service at one of his outlying parishes. A furious gale blew up and snow fell 'as if they were throwing it out of buckets'. The unfortunate cleric wandered around for over twenty-seven hours, even unwittingly managing to evade a search party. Eventually he found his way home, thankful for his 'most wonderful preservation'.

Above: Dawn mist rolling off Hazler Hill from the Long Mynd. [JC]

Right: Ashes Hollow with Ragleth Hill to the left. [JC]

The MALVERN HILLS,
Hereford and Worcester.
Much of the countryside
here is covenanted land,
rather than owned by the
National Trust. Protection
from development can be
provided by covenant: the
owner, after consultation
with the Trust, puts restrictions on the use of their
land, and such restrictions
remain with the deeds, even
if the land is sold or let.

To many, the Malverns are
the quintessential English
landscape, with their gentle,
quiet beauty, evoked by Sir
Edward Elgar in his music.
Right: Looking north to
the Worcestershire Beacon.
[JC]

The CLENT HILLS lie just south of Birmingham, providing the Black Country, in the words of Edgar Marriott's *Albert & the Lion*, with 'fresh air and fun'. *Right:* The sandstone hills, woody in parts, are steep but easy to climb, with superb views. [DN]

Far right: Looking towards the whaleback of the Malvern Hills (pp.68–9) rising abruptly from the Severn Plain. [DN]

CROOME PARK in Hereford and Worcester. Between 1747 and 1809 the 6th Earl of Coventry commissioned a series of leading garden designers and architects to lay out his landscape garden: Sanderson Miller, John Phipps, Lancelot 'Capability' Brown, Robert Adam and James Wyatt. But it is Brown's work, producing a 'natural landscape', that is most evident today.

In 1996 the National Trust purchased the central part of the parkland, which includes most of the significant parts of the landscape. Former grazing regimes are being reintroduced, including the reinstatement of the deer park, and restoration of the park to its early nineteenth-century appearance is underway. *Above:* View over the 'river', a serpentine lake, in early summer. [DN] *Right:* The landscape park with the Malvern Hills in the distance. [DN]

Following pages: Looking towards Croome Court, Capability Brown's earliest architectural work, 1751-2, probably following the designs of Sanderson Miller. [DN]

The way through the woods at Leigh, Bristol. The first section of LEIGH WOODS, within the city boundaries on the banks of the Avon, was given to the National Trust in 1909 by the Wills tobacco family, and other parts have been added over the years. Today it is a National Nature Reserve, where the Trust works in cooperation with English Nature, Forest Enterprise, and the Avon Community Forest to maintain the remains of a semi-natural ancient forest of wych elm, ash, oak, small-leaved lime and, uniquely, two species of whitebeam. [DN]

In 1944 Sir Richard Acland gave the National Trust all the land in his possession – the Holnicote Estate in Somerset of 12,400 acres (5,000 ha), and the Killerton Estate in Devon, of 6,400 acres (2,600 ha). At the time this gift roused considerable antagonism, and Sir Richard ruefully remarked that there was a feeling that donors were supposed to be dead. Now however, his gifts are much enjoyed by thousands of visitors, especially those to the Exmoor countryside of HOLNICOTE.

The Horner River, with its fine oak woods, rises on DUNKERY BEACON and runs through Exmoor National Park. [DN]

The view from BOSSINGTON HILL towards Porlock Bay. This picture, taken in 1993, is now out of date as the National Trust is undertaking managed retreat of the bay. As the shingle holding back the sea is breached, the farmland reverts to a saltmarsh habitat. [JC]

Above: WATERSMEET in Devon is so called because two rivers join here: the East Lyn and the Hoar Oak Water, with their oak hanging woodlands where for centuries coppicing took place to provide pit props for the coal mines of South Wales. From Watersmeet the united rivers flow swiftly to the sea at Lynmouth, beneath Lyn and Myrtleberry Cleave. This photograph shows the two Cleaves. [JC]

Right: Abandoned engine houses are connected irrevocably with the Cornish landscape and tin mining, but this example, WHEAL BETSY, is in Devon, and was used for lead mining. Set romantically on Black Down, on the west edge of Dartmoor, Wheal Betsy is a reminder that this area was once a heavily industrial site. [DN]

Above: The roofless engine house and stack of Towanroath Shaft, Wheal Coates. A track taken by the tin and copper miners descends from the dramatic clifftop site into the narrow cleft of CHAPEL PORTH on the north Cornish coast. This is the landscape described by Daphne du Maurier in *Vanishing Cornwall*. [JC]

Right: PENTIRE HEAD, a cliff headland bought in 1936 by public subscription to prevent the building of bungalows. This view looks towards the Rumps, a tiny peninsula projecting from the northern corner. The neck of the peninsula provides a splendid natural defence: in the Iron Age a castle was built here, and its fortifications can still be picked out as bumps in the turf. [JC]

Above: The path between the Rumps and PENTIRE POINT, forming just one part of the coastal footpath that leads the dedicated walker around the Cornish coast, 313 miles of dramatic changes in landscape. This is very much a stronghold for the National Trust, which protects about 130 miles, most of it acquired through its coastal appeal, Enterprise Neptune. [JC]

While the cliff headland of Pentire lies on the north coast, constantly exposed to the Atlantic, with hardy moorland vegetation, ST ANTHONY-IN-ROSELAND, on the south coast, enjoys a much kinder climate (*right*). This produces a gentler landscape of arrears, or flooded valleys that are havens for yachtsmen. This view from St Anthony's Head looks towards Great Malunan Beach. [JC]

Previous pages: FONTMELL DOWN in Dorset, taken in midsummer. This is Thomas Hardy country, and Fontmell was acquired by the National Trust in 1977 as a memorial to him. The chalk downlands provide habitats for butterflies, especially the small blue, common blue and chalk-hill blue, orchids and sheep-grazing flowers such as cowslips. [DN]

Right: BROWNSEA ISLAND lies in Europe's largest natural harbour, at Poole in Dorset. The peacock is sitting on a memorial commemorating the first camp set up here in 1907 by General Baden-Powell, from which sprang the Boy Scouts' Association. [JC]

There has been a settled community on Brownsea since prehistoric times, but perhaps the island's busiest period came in the nineteenth century when a pottery works was built on the north-west end, along with a workers' village named Maryland after the proprietor's wife. This village was largely abandoned when the island was bought by Mrs Bonham Christie in 1927. Opposed to blood sports and to the exploitation of animals by man in any form, she turned Brownsea into a wildlife sanctuary, now enjoyed by thousands of visitors.
Far right: Trees and ferns growing over the remains of Maryland. [JC]

This Stone Commemorates the experimental Camp of 20 boys held on this site from 1st–9th August 1907 by Robert Baden-Powell later Lord Baden-Powell of Gilwell Founder of the Scout and Guide Movements

AVEBURY in Wiltshire is perhaps the most important prehistoric monument in Europe, with a Neolithic causewayed enclosure at Windmill Hill, and a megalithic site of *c.*1800 BC that includes circles of sarsen stones enclosed by a bank and ditch, approached by an avenue of more stones. Unlike Stonehenge, where the stone circle stands isolated on a hill, at Avebury the medieval village is enmeshed with the stones, giving the impression that the houses are surrounded by a sculpture park (*above*). [DN]

That is not to say that Avebury lacks atmosphere. On a late winter's day, or at misty sunrise, the sarsen stones of the Avenue are a haunting sight (*right*). [DN]

Following pages: CHERHILL DOWN, overlooking the Vale of Pewsey, in Wiltshire. While the Vale is given over to large-scale arable farming, the downland above is a prehistoric landscape with tumuli, barrows, and strip-fields from an earlier agricultural system. The Trust takes care to maintain this landscape, using neither plough nor chemical spray and encouraging chalkland flowers which attract butterflies. To the right of the picture can be seen the Lansdowne Monument, built by the 3rd Marquess in 1845 in memory of the economist, Sir William Petty. Below is a fine white horse carved into the shoulder of the down. [DN]

: 94 : *Right:* VENTNOR DOWN, at the south-east end of the Isle of Wight. This is coastal heath laid on top of the chalk. The bracken provides sufficient cover for bluebells, which would normally not survive the competition with other more virulent sun-loving plants. [JC]

There has been a serious decline of traditional heathland habitats in south-east England over recent years because this type of landscape is particularly vulnerable to the development of scrub. The National Trust is reversing this decline by grazing the land and thus encouraging former habitats to return.

Above: Semi-wild New Forest ponies were recently introduced to VENTNOR DOWN. [JC]

Right: A similar solution is being applied at LUDSHOTT COMMON in Hampshire. [JC]

Previous pages: Sir Robert Hunter had fought many battles to save open spaces around London when he was Honorary Solicitor to the Commons Preservation Society in the 1860s, 70s and 80s. After he had helped to found the National Trust, he continued his efforts to protect open land, especially around Hindhead, close to his Surrey home. With its easy access by rail to London, this area was particularly desired for stockbroker development. In 1906 the Hindhead Preservation Committee bought up and presented to the Trust the Devil's Punch Bowl and Gibbet Hill, with Inval and Weydown Commons to the south-east. This photograph shows HINDHEAD COMMON from the Punch Bowl. [JC]

Right: The Gothic folly of LEITH HILL TOWER stands on the highest point in south-east England, with glorious views of the Weald and the South Downs. The slopes of the hill are wooded, with some stands of ancient oak and hazel amongst replanting. On the southern slopes is a rhododendron wood including many early-flowering species and hybrids, planted in the nineteenth century by Josiah Wedgwood, grandson of the famous potter. [JC]

Far right: GIBBET HILL rises to 895 feet above the Devil's Punch Bowl. It derives its name from a murder that took place on the old A3 road which can still be seen, now a quiet leafy lane, but once the main highway from Portsmouth to London. Here, in 1786, a sailor was set upon, robbed and left for dead. His three murderers were hanged on the top of the hill and then their corpses were preserved in tar and hung from the gibbet as a dire warning to others. [JC]

Left: Little Pond on FRENSHAM COMMON in Surrey. The presence of water in a sandy area is explained by the fact that this was an iron pan, used as a hammer pond when Frensham, on the edge of the Weald, was an industrial site in the seventeenth century.

Now the two ponds at Frensham are visited by migrant birds. The famous naturalist, Gilbert White of Selborne, recorded in a letter dated 7 May 1779, ' In the last week of last month, five of the most rare birds, too uncommon to have obtained an English name, but known to naturalists by the term of *himantopus* were shot upon the verge of Frensham Pond.... These birds are of the plover family, and might with propriety be called stilted plovers'. [JC]

Above: BOOKHAM COMMON is a large area of wooded common-land linked by a network of ancient routes. In the Middle Ages it belonged to the monks of Chertsey Abbey who grazed their pigs here and stored their fish in the ancient ponds. Now it is an area rich in natural history, renowned particularly for its insects, birds and wetland plants. [JC]

The ASHRIDGE ESTATE on the north-eastern end of the Chilterns in Hertfordshire consists of 4,000 acres (1,600 ha) of wonderfully varied landscape including farmland, common, down and woodland. It came to the National Trust in 1925 after Stanley Baldwin, then Prime Minister, made valiant appeals to the vendor's trustees, wealthy donors, and local people – including the children of the six village schools. Their response sealed the success of one of the great conservation campaigns of the day.

Right: One of the ancient pollarded trees that makes up Frithsden Beeches at Ashridge. [PW]

Far right: Grassy tracks invite walkers through the woods near Coldharbour Farm. [PW]

Previous pages: HATFIELD FOREST is the last remnant of the great medieval Forest of Essex, hunting preserve of the Norman kings. Just over 1,000 acres (400 ha) of woodland survive, broken up into sections separated by permanent wood banks and chases, wide grassy rides. The forest's long continuity has resulted in a wide variety of native trees and shrubs. This photograph shows three of the pollarded hornbeams that are such an important feature of the forest.

Left: Sunlight viewed through a horse chestnut. [PW]

Right: Looking through the branches of an ornamental plane tree. These trees provide habitats for a variety of rare insects. [PW]

One of the first properties discussed by the National Trust was WICKEN FEN in Cambridgeshire. Wicken represented the only substantial area of undrained East Anglian fenland. Its proximity to Cambridge meant that it had become an outdoor laboratory for enthusiastic entomologists, who were inadvertently destroying the very wildlife they sought to study. The first two plots of Wicken were bought in 1899, and the Trust duly acquired its first nature reserve.

Above: Pink hemp agrimony and white meadowsweet growing up through the common reed which lines Wicken Lode. The reed is the dominant species of the fens, cut annually for thatching. [PW]

Right: The pond viewed from the hide. With the help of the RSPB, the Trust has inaugurated a Fenland Restoration Project to encourage the proliferation of birds such as bittern, warblers, heron and water rail. [PW]

Overleaf: The Tower Hide at Wicken. This photograph shows a habitat now extremely rare in the fens, a 'litter' field. 'Litter' is a mixture of grasses and some reed which is cut every year, or once every two years, for hay. Such a regime provides a wealth of wild flowers: seen here are purple and yellow loosestrife and pink hemp agrimony. [PW]

Far right: DUNWICH HEATH in Suffolk, showing Docwra's Ditch, which is named after Jack Docwra, the warden who dug it in the late 1970s and 80s. The ditch acts as both a firebreak and a reservoir as the dry sandy heath-land, with its heather, bracken and silver birch, is very much at risk. Dunwich Heath lies next to the Royal Society for the Protection of Birds' major nature reserve at Minsmere, and is there-fore rich in birdlife, including the avocet, symbol of the RSPB. [JC]

Right: NORTHEY ISLAND, off the Essex coast. Here the Trust is taking part in an experiment with the Environment Agency and English Nature to allow the sea to breach the old defences and return the habitat to saltmarsh (see also p.79). This will not only encourage saltmarsh birds to overwinter, but also provide a buffer to protect other areas vulnerable to flooding. This photograph was taken twenty months after removal of the sea wall, and shows how quickly saltmarsh plants are establishing themselves. [JC]

ORFORD NESS is a narrow spit of shingle on the Suffolk coast, southwards from Alde-burgh. *Right:* The shingle surface preserves a complex pattern of ridges and swales (valleys) deposited over many centuries and recording stages in the evolution of the land form. This shingle provides a habitat for plants and seabirds, especially for the common gull: Orford has the largest breeding colony in Europe. [JC]

Above: The gulls make use of any material they can find for their nests on the shingle. [JC]

For the past century the flatness and isolated nature of Orford Ness has been exploited for military purposes. In the First World War, it was used by the Royal Flying Corps. During the 1930s Sir Robert Watson-Watt carried out the first experiments in radar. In the Second World War Barnes Wallis worked at Orford experimenting with new types of bombs. Finally, during the Cold War, the Atomic Weapons Research Establishment erected pagodas to test out various parts of nuclear bombs, while 'over the horizon' radar was installed on the Cobra Mist site.

In the 1970s, the Ness was declared surplus to Ministry of Defence requirements, and twenty years later, in 1993, a five mile stretch was bought by the National Trust through its coastal appeal, Enterprise Neptune, with the support of various organisations.

Right: Once more the Ness can be an area of wilderness for the avocet and the marsh harrier, rather than the bouncing bomb and other sinister projects. Already this photograph is out of date, with only the black tower left. [JC]

Far right: The estuarial mudflats at Orford, now home to thousands of waders. [JC]

: 120 : Sunset over the Ness, looking towards the little town of ORFORD. It was this bleak, uncompromising landscape that inspired the poetry of George Crabbe, and through him Benjamin Britten's opera, *Peter Grimes*. [JC]

DARNBROOK FARM in the North Yorkshire dales is a limestone landscape, eroded by the action of rain water. *Above:* A detail of limestone pavement on Cowside, with Darnbrook Fell in the distance. The clints and grykes are now protected under a 'limestone pavement order' to stop them being removed to garden centres, where they have proved all too popular. [JC]

Right: COWSIDE BECK, once grazed by cattle but now almost entirely given over to sheep. [JC]

Above: Limestone pavement and dry-stone walling at DARNBROOK. These walls are probably two or three hundred years old, constructed with stones cleared from the fields, and interlocked with no mortar but much skill. The National Trust organises working holidays to repair them. [JC]

Right: Ice formations on HARDCASTLE CRAGS, created by Hebden Water as it drains the Heptonstall and Wadsworth Moors of West Yorkshire and tumbles down to join the River Calder at the picturesque woollen town of Hebden Bridge.

Red squirrels can still be found in the woods of oak, larch and pine planted by the Savile family, and given to the National Trust in 1950. For years the Crags have been a green lung for the mill workers of Halifax and Rochdale. [JC]

: 126 : UPPER WHARFEDALE,
near Burnsall in North
Yorkshire, with a farm
nestling into its surround-
ings. The local limestone has
been used for its buildings
and for the dry-stone walls
that divide the fields: the
true meaning of vernacular
architecture.

Wharfedale has been
farmed since prehistoric
times, and the mosaic of
fields has been traditionally
used for a mixture of crops
and sheep grazing. The
National Trust owns eight
upland farms, a former deer
park, and stands of ancient
oak woodland on the valley
sides. The traditional way of
farming has been allowed
to continue, preserving
unimproved pasture and
wildflower meadows. [DN]

ROSEBERRY COMMON in autumn and icy midwinter.
Above: Harvested fields at Little Ayton, with the pyramidal
outline of Roseberry Topping, rising 1,057 feet above sea level,
providing a picturesquely named and familiar landmark for the
heavily populated area of Teeside. [JC]

Right: Snowdrifts in the lee of dry-stone walls, with Roseberry
Topping on the right and the Cleveland Hills beyond. [JC]

: 130 : Marsden Moor in West Yorkshire forms part of the Peak District and the scenery for BBC TV's *Last of the Summer Wine.* Here shown in bleak midwinter, in summer its bleakness is not greatly diminished, with a peat blanket providing habitat for mosses and moorland grasses, for curlew and golden plover. [JC]

HORDEN on the Durham coal coast marks a watershed for the National Trust's coastal appeal, Enterprise Neptune. To celebrate Neptune's 500th mile in 1988, the Trust bought the coal blackened beach in front of the site of the former Easington Colliery from British Coal for £1.

Coal had been extracted from seams running under the seabed, and the waste or slag tipped on the beach, where much of it was washed out to sea. In places the slag formed a layer many yards deep, completely obliterating the coastal landscape. Since the closure of the collieries, Mother Nature, with man's help, has carried out a remarkable 'clean up' which has almost restored the beach to its pre-mining condition. Today this area of coast is once again teeming with wildlife, and a popular attraction for visitors.

Above: The view along Horden Beach north to Beacon Hill. [JC]

Left: Wildflowers growing in meadowland at Beacon Point. [JC]

Whin Sill is a volcanic, doleritic ridge providing a formidably effective barrier for the Romans to construct HADRIAN'S WALL, and running through to the Farne Islands off the Northumbrian coast. This photograph shows Crag Lough, one of a series of little loughs below the Sill, with stands of common reed (*Phragmites australis*). [PW]

Right: SYCAMORE GAP on Hadrian's Wall. This tree took a starring role in Kevin Costner's film, *Robin Hood, Prince of Thieves.* [JC]

Far right: The Roman fort of Housesteads on HADRIAN'S WALL, looking out towards Sewingshields Crags. In the foreground is the South Granary: the stone piers supported wooden ventilated flooring for the storage of grain. [PW]

Following pages: When the Emperor Hadrian ordered the building of a wall from the Solway Firth to the mouth of the Tyne in AD 122, the Roman Empire was at its height, stretching from this northern out-post east to what is now Iraq, and south to the Sahara Desert. Whin Sill provided a craggy northern face to set against the Picts; the gentler southern slopes led toward the civilised world. This photograph shows part of the most dramatic section of HADRIAN'S WALL, winding its way across the landscape, with the blue of Crag Lough in the distance. [PW]

Joe Cornish

Joe Cornish was born and educated in Devon, before studying fine arts at Reading University. He worked as photographic assistant first to Mike Mitchell in Washington, and then with Dave Hart and Dale McAfee in London. His first 'clients' were actors and musicians for whom he did promotional portraits, but his customer list now includes many book publishers, magazines and organisations such as the Countryside Commission, the Cleveland Wildlife Trust and the Heritage Lottery Fund. The first book to which he contributed the photography was *Founders of the National Trust* published by Christopher Helm. He has also worked on books about France, Italy, and several guidebooks for Dorling Kindersley. He now lives in North Yorkshire.

Originally inspired by family holidays spent on the north Cornish coast, he has come particularly to enjoy photographing landscapes. The work of American masters like Ansel Adams and Edward Weston has given him a reverence for nature and in particular unspoilt, wilderness areas. Britain, in fact, is virtually wilderness free, but he identifies the coast below the high-tide mark as offering an authentic taste of untamed nature, where the ebb and flow of the sea will always resist man's efforts to domesticate. The ancient mountain landscapes of western and northern Britain evoke for him a sense of age and history combined with textural and colour subtlety that is often absent from younger, higher mountain ranges, such as the European Alps.

Joe decided he would like to work for the National Trust's Photographic Library after his involvement in the book on the founders. To celebrate the twenty-fifth anniversary of the launch of the coastal appeal, Enterprise Neptune, in 1990 the Trust commissioned the writer Charlie Pye-Smith to write *In Search of Neptune*, and Joe took the photographs. Since then he has travelled all over England, Wales and Northern Ireland for the Trust: 'To me, the Trust's landscape work is a force for our current benefit and for that of future generations. It follows therefore, that I feel my job is to express that work in the most evocative and positive way possible. Whenever I can, I take my photographs at dawn or dusk, exploiting the beautiful light conditions which tend to arise then if the weather is right.'

He started with 35mm SLRs, and still uses 35mm - he has Nikons with a range of lenses - but tends to limit their use to documentary-style portraits and general travel subjects. For landscape photographs he originally bought a second-hand Rolleicord twin lens reflex 6x6 (medium format) camera, replaced first by a Rolleiflex SLX single lens reflex, and then by a Pentax 6x7. Experience taught him to have extremely tough, reliable gear - the Pentax, for instance, stopped working after a close encounter with a large wave on the Cobb at Lyme Regis in Dorset. By 1986 therefore he had come down to two cameras, a Hasselblad 500CM and a Plaubel 69W Proshift, a fixed lens wide-angle camera with a built-in shift frame, and has used these ever since for his National Trust work. He continues to experiment and is currently working with a Horseman 612 camera for landscape work.

In the 1970s Kodachrome 64 (&25) was virtually *de rigueur* for anybody shooting 35mm. As it wasn't available in medium format film, he used Ektachrome 64 and later Fujichrome 50, until the arrival of Fuji Velvia in 1990. It is intolerant of exposure error, however, and slower than the 50 ASA stated. For shorter exposure and late twilight he uses Provia 100.

David Noton was born in Bedfordshire but emigrated soon after to California. A peripatetic childhood spent in the UK and Canada was followed by a career in the Merchant Navy. His interest in photography began at sea, and in 1982 he returned to college in Gloucester. During his final year he sold Athena a range of images for publication as posters, which proved a springboard for going freelance. Initially his work was a balance of landscape and local commercial commissions for advertising agencies, design groups and public relations companies in the west country, from his Bristol base. By the 1990s his main activity was stock photography in the fields of landscape, nature and travel, and clients included NatWest, the National Grid, Ikea, the BBC Natural History Unit and the National Trust. He has won awards in the landscape categories of the British Gas/BBC Wildlife Photography Competition in 1985, 1990 and 1991. He is now based in Sherborne, Dorset.

As a keen walker and mountaineer, landscape photography was perhaps a natural preference which has endured. The Scottish Highlands and Islands were where his earliest photographic forays took place, and is still one of his favourite places. He relishes the ambience and unpredictability of field-work.

Despite, or perhaps as a result of travelling all over the world, David appreciates the wealth of differing landscapes - from dramatic mountain ranges to pastoral rolling farmland - offered by the British Isles. Because of the northerly latitude and the changeable weather, the subtlety of the light is unique. Man's imprint on the landscape, for instance the dry-stone walling and farm buildings in the Yorkshire Dales, adds visual harmony: 'Straight off the plane from, say, North America the patchwork of green fields still hits me between the eyes.'

The National Trust's Photographic Library is his longest running client, a relationship that started in 1986. The organisation is an obvious port of call for a photographer as it manages some of the most beautiful landscapes in Britain. 'To be able again and again to experience nature at its most enchanting at dawn on Derwentwater in the Lakes, or as storm waves crash on the rugged coast of the Lizard Peninsula in Cornwall brings home in no uncertain terms what a treasure we have in our landscape. I am committed to the work the Trust does in protecting these areas, and if in a small way my photographs help with that mission, it gives me great satisfaction.'

In the past ten years, David has used a whole range of equipment, but lately his set-up is Nikon 35mm gear and a Fuji 6x17cm panoramic camera. He is committed to the flexibility of 35mm, while appreciating the more considered but less spontaneous approach of working on the large 617 format. Virtually all his colour work is shot on Fuji Velvia.

Paul Wakefield was born in Hong Kong, educated there and in the UK, and studied photography at Bournemouth and Birmingham Colleges of Art. He started his career as a photographer by freelancing for publishers, design groups and record companies while still at college. He now works mainly in advertising, with clients like car companies, British Gas, Smirnoff and Johnnie Walker. His exhibitions include the Photographers' Gallery in 1984, Gallery of Photography Dublin in 1991 and the Saatchi Gallery in 1994. Publications include three collaborations with Jan Morris on the landscapes of Wales, Scotland and Ireland. In 1997 he was given the Gold Award from the Association of Photo-graphers. His studios are based in London.

Paul's interest in landscape stems from walking in the Hong Kong countryside with his father and brothers. He spends as much time as possible photographing for himself, and has most recently been working in Patagonia and the United States. He began working with the National Trust's Photographic Library about five years ago.

For cameras he uses a Linhof 5x4, Fuji 6x17/ 6x9 and a Leica M6. For colour film he uses Fuji Velvia, and for black and white shots, Agfapan 25/100.

The Coast
of England, Wales, and Northern Ireland

INTRODUCTION BY LIBBY PURVES

JOE CORNISH · PAUL WAKEFIELD · DAVID NOTON

IN THE SAME SERIES FROM THE NATIONAL TRUST:

Coast

A photographic tour around the coast of England, Wales and Northern Ireland,
as seen through the lenses of three leading landscape photographers:
Joe Cornish, David Noton and Paul Wakefield, with an introduction by Libby Purves.
ISBN 0-8109-6360-4

Photographic books on gardens and historic house interiors
are planned for publication in 1999.

About the National Trust

The National Trust is Europe's leading conservation charity, looking after over 673,000 acres (272,000 ha) of countryside, 570 miles of coastline, 263 historic houses and 233 gardens and parks in England, Wales and Northern Ireland. The Trust continually requires funds to meet its responsibility of maintaining all these properties for the benefit of the nation. To find out how you can help, please contact:
The National Trust, 36 Queen Anne's Gate, London, SW1H 9AS (0171 222 9251).

Enterprise Neptune

Since 1965 when this special appeal was launched, the Enterprise Neptune campaign has acquired some of the finest – and often most vulnerable – coastal areas of England, Wales and Northern Ireland for permanent preservation by the National Trust. For more information contact:
The Enterprise Neptune Office, Attingham Park, Shrewsbury, Shropshire SY4 4TP (01743 709 343).

Membership

Joining the National Trust will give you free entry to properties and directly funds the Trust's work. For details of how to join, contact:
The National Trust Membership Department, PO Box 39, Bromley, Kent BR1 1NH (0181 315 1111).

Legacies

Please consider leaving the Trust a legacy in your will. All legacies to the National Trust are used either for capital expenditure at existing properties or for the purchase or endowment of new property – not for administration. For more information contact:
The Head of Legacies Unit, 36 Queen Anne's Gate, London SW1H 9AS (0171 222 9251).

The Royal Oak Foundation

This US not-for-profit membership organisation supports the National Trust's activities in areas of special interest to Americans. For membership and programme information in the US contact:
The Royal Oak Foundation, 285 West Broadway, New York, NY 10013 USA (00 1 212 966 6565).